D1240652

Shooting Star

By Margaret Beames

Illustrated by Kelvin Hawley

DOMINIE PRESS

Pearson Learning Group

Publisher: Raymond Yuen
Project Editor: John S. F. Graham
Editor: Bob Rowland
Designer: Greg DiGenti
Illustrator: Kelvin Hawley

Published by:

℗ Dominie Press, Inc.

1949 Kellogg Avenue
Carlsbad, California 92008 USA

www.dominie.com

1-800-232-4570

Paperback ISBN 0-7685-1821-0
Printed in Singapore
8 9 10 09 08

Table of Contents

Chapter One

I Am Not an It

A bright star shot across the night sky.
It followed the normal trail that a
shooting star would follow. But then it
suddenly dropped over a small hill in the
middle of a small town. It landed so hard
that it made a hole ten feet deep. A wisp

of steam rose from the hole. Then—nothing.

Daylight came. Andy woke up early. And, because he couldn't bear to stay in bed a moment longer on such a beautiful day, he got up and went outside.

He ran along the road to the park. He knew that park better than anything. He climbed the little hill in the middle of it, like he always did. But then he stopped in amazement. There was a hole in the ground that hadn't been there before!

He peered down into it. To his surprise, a small face with large, shining eyes and wide, pointed ears looked back up at him. It was some kind of creature. When it saw Andy, it held up its arms as if to say, "Lift me out!"

Andy stumbled backward. Did he really see what he just saw? He decided

to have a look again.

The big eyes were still looking up at him. They looked right into his eyes. Then a strange feeling shot through his head, as if something was right there inside it—reading him like a book!

Then he heard a voice. "Hello," it said. "Can you understand me? Are you a human?" It was a girl's voice.

Andy gulped. It was talking to him. "Yes," he said. "I'm Andy."

"You are very small. I thought humans were big," the voice said.

"I'm only seven," said Andy. "I haven't finished growing." Andy was a little puzzled. He saw where the creature was, but the voice was coming from inside his own head. "How can it talk into my head?" he thought. "How does it do that?"

"This way is better," the voice said.

"Oh, great. It can read my mind," thought Andy. "I'd better be careful what I think! I wonder where it came from?"

"You do not know my planet," the little creature said. "I only wanted to fly over and have a look, but I came too close. I crashed, and my spaceship is broken. I am still learning. Can you help me?"

"Well," thought Andy, "it seems harmless enough. And I can't let it stay in the hole."

"Thank you," the creature said, reading his mind again. "And I am not an *It*. I am *Tiggy*."

Chapter Two
Show Me Your Town

Andy looked around and found a dead branch under a nearby bush. It was just long enough for Tiggy to reach the end and hang on with long, bony fingers.

Tiggy climbed the rest of the way out of the hole and stood next to Andy. She was smaller than he thought. She came up just to Andy's shoulder. Her head was large for her wispy little body. She was very strange, but he liked her. He decided he should look after her. There was no way she could get home with her spaceship broken.

"Someone will come for me," she said, "when it is dark." Her voice was in his head again. "Now I will look at your world." She began to walk down the hill.

"Hey," he said. "You can't just walk around like that!" Andy cried. "If anyone sees you, they'll call the cops. They'll lock you up, do experiments, and all kinds of crazy stuff."

"That is not a problem," Tiggy remarked. "No one will see me."

"How—" Then Andy gasped. Tiggy was gone. In her place was only a wavy,

hazy mist. Then that vanished, too.

"It is easy to disappear when you know how," said her voice.

"Wow," Andy said. "What about your spaceship?"

"What spaceship?" Tiggy said.

Andy looked back to see that the hole—and the ship—were gone. He didn't know what Tiggy's smile might look like, but he thought she was smiling just then.

"Now," Tiggy said, "show me your town."

Chapter Three
Turn It Off!

Andy looked down the hill. He saw the sun shining on the railroad tracks. It was almost time for the morning train to go through. He could show that to Tiggy. "Here's something," he said.

The railroad crossing arms were down

to stop cars from going through, and the red lights were flashing. Then the bell started ringing.

"Turn it off!" Tiggy's voice shrieked inside Andy's head.

"I can't," he yelled over the noise. "It'll stop as soon as the train has gone by. Here it comes."

The train thundered past with a terrifying howl of its horn.

"What was that terrible thing?" she asked. Andy could feel Tiggy's pain in his own head.

"Don't think so hard," he protested. "It hurts."

He was about to explain about trains, when he noticed some people giving him strange looks. He was talking to her out loud, but she was silent, not to mention invisible. "Come on," he thought hastily.

"We'll go look at the stores."

He led her to a street corner with a traffic light and a crosswalk.

"What are stores?" she asked. "And what are those big metal things rushing past? Why have we stopped?"

She was asking all sorts of questions.

"We cross the street when we see a little green man," Andy told her.

"Green? Where?"

"Careful!" Andy warned her. He could see a hazy shape beside him. She was looking all around for a green man, her bat-like ears twitching wildly. Then she disappeared again. Andy hoped no one had noticed. A little girl was staring at him, but just at that moment a huge truck roared by, going faster than it should have been and leaving behind a trail of oily, black smoke.

Tiggy screamed, which filled Andy's ears from the inside. Before he could tell her everything was OK, a police car with its siren wailing raced past after the speeding truck. Then in the air above, a deafening roar came down from the sky.

Chapter Four
Staring and Pointing

"It's only a jet..." Andy began. *Oh, no!* He could see her! And so could everyone else. People were staring and pointing.

"Hey, kid, who is that with you?" a police officer shouted.

"Nothing! I mean it's a... she's a... This

19

is my little sister in a costume. That's all."
He tried to stay calm, but he couldn't.
Neither could Tiggy. She ran away in a
strange kind of leap-skip-leap high into
the air that no small child would ever do.
Andy ran after her, trying to catch up.

"People can see you!" Andy gasped.

"Oops!" said Tiggy, and she
disappeared as she ran.

Andy heard shouts behind him. "What
kind of a costume is that? Hey, kid, stop!
Catch them!"

Andy ran as fast as he could down the
street. He couldn't see Tiggy, but
somehow he knew she was still there.
He knew the people behind him had
seen her, and even worse, they had seen
her disappear. They didn't believe she
was his little sister in a costume. And
now the police knew about her.

Andy and Tiggy passed a group of construction workers who were using jackhammers to dig up the street.

"Quick," he said, almost out of breath. "Let's go in here." They turned quickly and went into an arcade. Coin-operated games blew strange noises at them. Loud music came blaring down from speakers in the ceiling.

"I think we lost them," Andy said.

Tiggy started appearing, then disappearing, then reappearing. Andy could tell she was afraid and upset.

"Too much noise!" she said.

They sat down in a quieter area of the arcade. At least, Andy thought it was quieter.

"My planet is much calmer," Tiggy said. "There is so much activity here."

"You have to be careful and look out

for things," Andy said. "Something or another is going on all the time. You have to be aware."

Tiggy stopped disappearing and looked around. "Why were those people chasing us?"

Andy shrugged. "I don't know. Some people think that strange things are bad."

"Does that mean I am a strange thing?" Tiggy asked.

"No," Andy said. "Not to me. We're friends."

Tiggy smiled her Tiggy-like smile, but Andy could see that she was still bothered by the noise. She was shivering.

"Let's go someplace where there isn't as much noise," Andy said.

"I think I should go back to my spaceship," Tiggy said.

"OK," Andy said. He got up and

looked up and down the street. No one was around. "Remember to stay invisible this time," he told her.

Chapter Five

I Guess We're Used to It

It was better under the trees, but Tiggy seemed tired and sleepy. Andy was worried. Was she sick?

"It is the noise." Her voice was just a whisper now. Her ears were folded close against her head. "How can you live

here? It is too noisy."

"I guess we're used to it," Andy said.

Andy was hungry. He hadn't had breakfast. Did Tiggy need food?

"Not your food," Tiggy said. "I will eat when my ship comes tonight. I believe I will stay here. It is much quieter and nicer."

"I like it here, too," Andy said.

"I hope you do not get into trouble because of me," Tiggy said.

"Don't worry about it," Andy said. "I can talk my way out of anything."

Andy did not like to leave her, but he could not stay there all day. Soon his mother would wonder where he was.

"Go. I will be safe," she told him. "I can hide when I want to, remember?"

Andy nodded.

"Look for a bright light in the sky tonight," she said. "I do not like saying goodbye. Do not say goodbye to me now. We can say goodbye then."

"I'll miss you," Andy said.

Tiggy smiled, sort of. It looked like it might be a smile. Andy smiled back.

That night, Andy stood by his window. A brilliant light shot across the sky. "Look, a shooting star," said his mother. Andy smiled. He knew better.

"Goodbye, Tiggy. Good luck," he thought.

Then, into his head came a distant voice. "Goodbye, Andy, and thank you."